The Dalai Lama

by Sheila Rivera

Lerner Books • London • New York • Minneapolis

Photo Acknowledgements

The photographs in this book are reproduced with the permission of: © C Geral/Retna Ltd., front and back covers; © JAYANTA SHAW/Reuters/Corbis, p 4; © Toronto Star/ZUMA Press, pp 6, 7; © PETER PARKS/AFP/Getty Images, p 8; The Collection of the Newark Museum, p 9; © istockphoto.com/Xiaoping Liang, p 10; © Christine Kolisch/CORBIS, p 11; © CORBIS, p 12; © Earl & Nazima Kowall/CORBIS, p 13; © Bettmann/CORBIS, pp 14, 18, 19, 22; © Hulton-Deutsch Collection/CORBIS, p 16; AP/Wide World Photos, pp 17, 20, 24; © DAVID BEBBER/ Reuters/Corbis, p 25; © STRDEL/AFP/Getty Images, p 26.

First published in the United Kingdom in 2009 by
Lerner Books,
Dalton House,
60 Windsor Avenue,
London SW19 2RR

Website address: www.lernerbooks.co.uk

This edition was updated and edited for UK publication by Discovery Books Ltd., First Floor, 2 College Street, Ludlow, Shropshire SY8 1AN

Words in **bold type** are explained in a glossary on page 31.

British Library Cataloguing in Publication Data

Rivera, Sheila, 1970-
    The Dalai Lama - 2nd ed. - (Pull
    ahead books. Biographies)
    1. Bstan-dzin-rgya-mtsho, Dalai Lama XIV, 1935- - Juvenile
    literature 2. Dalai lamas - Biography - Juvenile literature
    I. Title
    294.3'923'092

    ISBN-13: 978 0 7613 4377 6

Printed in Singapore

Table of Contents

The Dalai Lama

Becoming a Leader

Do you know who the Dalai Lama is? He is the leader of Tibet. He is also a **religious** leader. The Dalai Lama is a **compassionate** person. He cares about people. He worries when people don't get along with each other. He believes in peace.

The Dalai Lama was born in a small town in Tibet. His parents named him Lhamo Dhondup.

Lhamo Dhondup

When Lhamo was a little boy, some **Buddhist monks** came to his house. These religious men knew that Lhamo was special.

Lhamo's parents took him to live with the monks in a **monastery**. This is where monks live and work together.

A monk walks in the monastery where the Dalai Lama lived.

Tibet's government announced that Lhamo was the Dalai Lama. He became the country's religious leader.

The Potala Palace

Two years later, the Dalai Lama went to live at the Potala Palace.

The Dalai Lama spent most of his time studying. He studied religion, art and many other subjects.

The Dalai Lama learned about this god when he studied religion.

The Dalai Lama liked to talk with the servants at the palace. They told him about the lives of ordinary Tibetans.

A group of Tibetans gather near the palace.

The Dalai Lama could see most of the town from the palace.

The Dalai Lama watched the people in town from his window. He cared about them very much.

Chinese soldiers moved into Tibet.

Danger

In 1950, China sent **soldiers** to Tibet. They said they would protect the Tibetans from other countries. But the Tibetan people thought that China wanted to rule Tibet.

The Dalai Lama was only 15 years old. But he became the head of Tibet's **government**. He wanted to keep Tibetans safe.

The Dalai Lama sits on his throne.

The Dalai Lama meets with China's leader, Mao Zedong in 1954.

He met with Chinese leaders. He talked about peace between China and Tibet.

Chinese soldiers force Tibetans to leave the palace.

The Chinese said they would help Tibet become a better country. But they did not help.

Chinese leaders said Tibet was part of China. They wanted to rule Tibet.

Soldiers in Tibet carry the Chinese flag.

The Dalai Lama (on the white horse) left Tibet.

Leaving Tibet

People were afraid that the Chinese soldiers would hurt the Dalai Lama. So he decided to move to India with his family. They would be safe in India. But the Dalai Lama still wanted to help his people in Tibet. He did not want them to suffer under Chinese rule.

Chinese soldiers stand guard in Tibet.

Talk of Peace

The Dalai Lama wanted the Chinese soldiers to leave Tibet. He wanted Tibet to be free again. But he did not want his people to fight. The Dalai Lama believed that **violence** was wrong.

The Dalai Lama talked to leaders from other countries. He asked them to help Tibet become free again.

The Dalai Lama asked US president Bill Clinton for help.

A group in Great Britain shows its support for Tibet.

People around the world urged the Chinese to let Tibet rule itself. But the Chinese would not.

The Dalai Lama teaches people to respect one another.

Love One Another

China still controls Tibet. The Dalai
Lama hopes that Tibet will be a free
country again one day. But he tells
Tibetans not to fight. He believes that
all people should love and care for one
another. He believes in compassion for
all people.

Dalai Lama Timeline

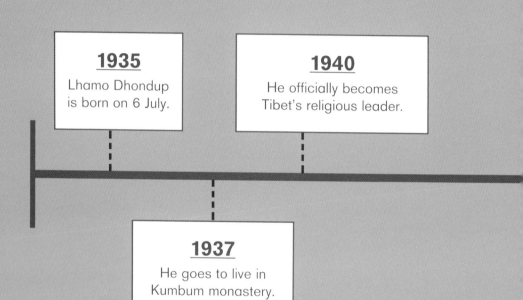

1935
Lhamo Dhondup is born on 6 July.

1940
He officially becomes Tibet's religious leader.

1937
He goes to live in Kumbum monastery.

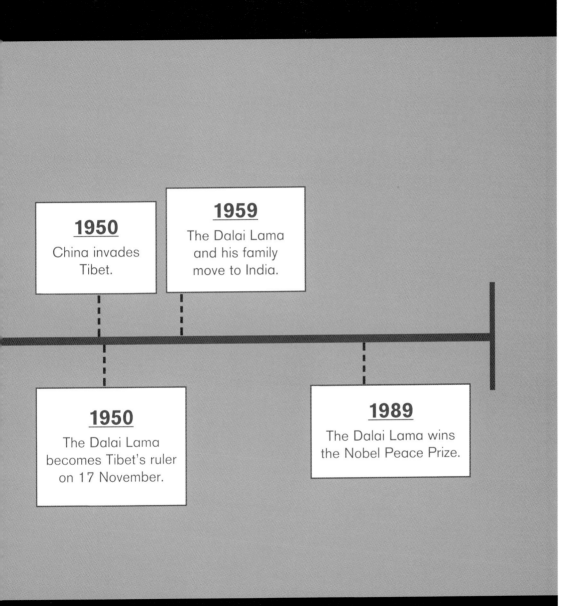

1950
China invades Tibet.

1959
The Dalai Lama and his family move to India.

1950
The Dalai Lama becomes Tibet's ruler on 17 November.

1989
The Dalai Lama wins the Nobel Peace Prize.

More about the Dalai Lama

● The Dalai Lama won the Nobel Peace Prize in 1989 for his work towards peace.

● The Tibetan people still consider the Dalai Lama their leader even though China controls Tibet.

● The Dalai Lama has lived in India for more than 45 years.

Glossary

Buddhist monks: men who give up everything to serve the Buddhist religion

compassionate: sharing someone else's suffering and wanting to help them

government: a group of people who run a country

monastery: a place where monks live and work

religious: believing in and worshipping a god or gods

soldiers: members of an army

violence: using physical force to damage or hurt people or things

Index

First published in the United States of America in 2007
Text copyright © 2007 by Lerner Publishing Group, Inc.